Trudeau Stories

Trudeau Stories

Brooke Johnson

Trudeau Stories
first published 2014 by
Scirocco Drama
An imprint of J. Gordon Shillingford Publishing Inc.

Scirocco Drama Editor: Glenda MacFarlane
Cover design by Terry Gallagher/Doowah Design Inc.
Cover photo is of Brooke Johnson and Pierre Elliott Trudeau, 1985. Used courtesy of the National Theatre School of Canada. Thanks to Gerry Porter in pre-press treatment.
Author photo by Adrian Truss
Production photos by R. Kelly Clipperton
Printed and bound in Canada on 100% post-consumer recycled paper.
An earlier version of *Trudeau Stories* was originally published in a limited edition chapbook format in 2012.

We acknowledge the financial support of the Manitoba Arts Council and The Canada Council for the Arts for our publishing program.

Production inquiries should be addressed to:
Brooke Johnson
c/o Long Black Car Productions
193A Roncesvalles Ave.
Toronto, ON M6R 2L5
info@trudeaustories.com

Library and Archives Canada Cataloguing in Publication

Johnson, Brooke, 1962-, author
Trudeau stories / Brooke Johnson.

A play.
ISBN 978-1-927922-04-0 (pbk.)

1. Trudeau, Pierre Elliott, 1919-2000--Drama. 2. Johnson, Brooke, 1962- –Drama. I. Title.

PS8569.O273T78 2014 C812'.54 C2014-903420-2

J. Gordon Shillingford Publishing
P.O. Box 86, RPO Corydon Avenue, Winnipeg, MB Canada R3M 3S3

Production History

Trudeau Stories was first performed as part of the Summerworks Theatre Festival in Toronto, August, 2007 at the Tarragon Theatre Mainspace, with the following cast and crew:

Brooke Johnson as herself & others

Directed by Allyson McMackon

Stage Manager: Fiona Jones

Technical Team: Shanna Miller, Verne Good, Gavin Fearon

Floor by Lindsay Anne Black, inspired by Ernest Cormier

Produced by Adrian Truss / Black Dog Group

Trudeau Stories was remounted by Theatre Passe Muraille, presented in the TPM Mainspace, Toronto, November, 2008 with the following cast and crew:

Brooke Johnson as herself & others

Directed by Allyson McMackon

Stage Manager: Fiona Jones

Lighting Design: Sarah Yaffe

Production Manager: Ryan McDougall

House Technician: Peter Eaton

Floor by Lindsay Anne Black, inspired by Ernest Cormier

Since July 2009, the play has been produced by Long Black Car Productions, with a lighting design by Glenn Davidson.

The playwright acknowledges the Ontario Arts Council and the Toronto Arts Council for workshop funding.

Brooke Johnson

Brooke is a 1987 graduate of the Acting Program of the National Theatre School of Canada, and has performed in theatres from Signal Hill to the Yukon River, from the National Arts Centre to the Georgia Strait. Amongst other acting honours, she has two Gemini Awards, and four Dora Mavor Moore nominations, and has enjoyed roles in the premieres of many new Canadian plays.

Trudeau Stories is her first written work for the stage. She also wrote and illustrated a children's book, *Uh Poo Fem Bon Furtz,* and with her partner, Adrian Truss, made a documentary entitled, *Massanoga,* about her grandfather's lumber mills in eastern Ontario.

She lives in Toronto, although during the summer months she is somewhere on the water in the Grand Banks trawler, *Mary Mary,* which she and Adrian sailed up the Intracoastal Waterway from the Gulf of Mexico.

The Origins of *Trudeau Stories*

Pierre Elliott Trudeau died in the late September of 2000. The grief I felt was in part shared publicly by millions of people, and in part it was desolately private. When I started to write what was subsequently filed in a folder and hastily labeled *Trudeau Stories*, it was out of the necessity of mourning. I wasn't writing a play or a book or even an article, but for myself, for remembrance. I needed to revisit a magical time in Montreal—sort it, see it in black and white, and so move out of my head what had been intensely personal. After the funeral, I started to sift through the memories, culling from scribblings in old notebooks and on napkins, on cardboard coasters and paper placemats; writing the memories of visits together as I rediscovered them. And it was a *re*discovery. I found in my old papers so much that I had forgotten. What we do as artists is share ourselves in one way or another, and I began to suspect that this folder labeled "Trudeau Stories" contained something of me which might be worth sharing.

In the darkest months of 2001, I asked Ross Manson, of Volcano Theatre, if I could read something at his quarterly event, *Short Stuff for Hot Writers*, and that spring shakily read the first drafts of two stories, "The Shoes" and "The Long Black Car". Much later, in 2004, the folks at Theatre Columbus asked if I had anything to show at *Mayhem* (their fundraising evenings of works-in-exploration) and so, having done nothing with the stories since *Short Stuff*, I extracted them from the filing cabinet and reworked them.

As an artist, I can't think that I had ever been more terrified than when I read those pieces aloud. I hadn't before exposed myself publicly as a writer; rather, I'd interpreted other people's writing, as an actor. I was also afraid, due to the subject matter, that sharing these memories would appear to be merely an exercise in self-aggrandisement. (It was partly that concern that had caused me keep this friendship to myself all these years.) The response I received at *Mayhem* was as much encouragement about the writing as it was excitement over the subject matter. It encouraged me that I had found a way to share my specific history in a way that had resonance.

But how to make it a play? The answer to that came, after some insightful editing from my partner, Adrian Truss, through a two week workshop and a subsequent physical rehearsal with Allyson McMackon of Theatre Rusticle, and Stage Manager / Font of Knowledge, my friend Fiona Jones. Allyson, through her particular genius, was able to grab hold of a shrugged-off impulse here and to mine what was a casually discarded thought over there, and, without too much polishing, reveal a sparkling insight. She deftly coaxed and elicited gesture and movement, helping me raise the words from the page while plucking and culling from the file folder, until a kind of circle of memories was woven of words and physicality.

Theatre and memory are entwined in so many ways. When I perform the play—in that wondrous conjuring way of live theatre—by sharing with an audience the Pierre Trudeau that I knew, I spend an hour or so with him again.

Oddly enough for a first-time playwright, I never considered that someone other than myself might perform this play.

At the time of this printing, I'll have performed it roughly 170 times in a variety of venues across Canada. Often there will be a talk-back afterwards and, occasionally, an audience member will ask if I'd ever actually had the opportunity to meet Pierre Trudeau. And I answer, as gently and clearly as I can, that while it may seem at times like a fairy tale, every line in the play is true (except that the gravy ladle was discovered *after* we went to the rooftop, not before—you'll know what I mean when you get there).

And sometimes, someone will ask me if I ever actually met Brooke Johnson. One man was quite generous about my ability as an actor, and enthused, "You were just like her. You were just like Brooke!"

And so, I have come around to the idea that perhaps someone else may as well play me.

But I've also been driven to wonder about the telling of stories. We are conditioned to the likelihood of invention: if it's up on stage with lights and props, the story must be a creation of the imagination. There is conjecture that the original Theatre was that of the hunter's clan. Let's say, just to contain the analogy, that the hunter's name was "Bruuk", and the whole clan was perched around the post-feast fire hearing the story of the hunt. These listeners wouldn't have said at that time: "But Bruuk, did you ever actually bag a deer?" because they'd have just eaten it. However, they may have wondered about the part in the story where Bruuk wrestled the monstrous bear at the edge of the gorge…

Here, although there is a poetic and fantastic quality to some of the following (and perhaps allusions to *Cinderella*) what with the beavers, the wild McGill boys and in fact, a deer or two, everything in the following pages is true.

If you wish to present the play, I suggest that while the CBC Archives is a rich resource for looking at and listening to recordings of Pierre Trudeau the politician, that you might take clues from the script to reimagine a rather soft-spoken, introspective man, possessed of keen curiosity, vulnerability, warmth and humour.

And, while you will find plenty of clues to my character within, my guess is that if you can find a way to portray your own true self, you will fulfill the intentions of the author.

—Brooke Johnson
September 2014

Some Script References that might be handy (there are more at the back of the book):

Mr. Dressup was a Canadian television program for children (CBC 1967-1996) as was *Chez Hélène* (CBC 1959-1973) and *The Friendly Giant* (CBC 1958-1985). "Rusty" was a puppet rooster who played a harp and lived in a sack which hung by Friendly's castle window.

Lost in the Barrens is a 1956 novel by Farley Mowat. *Of the Fields, Lately* is by Canadian playwright David French; the Jim Harrison quote is from his novella, *Legends of the Fall*. In one of his letters, Trudeau paraphrases Robert Browning's poem, "How They Brought the Good News from Ghent to Aix."

There are two telephone messages from Pierre Trudeau in the play. These messages were recorded on a cassette-style answering machine during the winter of 1992. If you would like to hear them or use them in a production, please send an email to: info@trudeaustories.com

The Stories

Seabreeze

(Enter with Seabreeze Journal)

This is a little book of mine I recently rediscovered. It's just a cheap Chinatown journal I'd picked up on a trip back to Montreal in 2002. I had wanted to jot down some thoughts. This is one of them:

I'm up here on the Terrasse of the Hotel de la Montagne. Forty years old now, almost to the day. (What's a couple of weeks in a fifteen year memory?)

I remember: Sitting at that table there, where three businessmen now sit bemoaning Nortel: "Ah", one of them says, "it's still in my RRSP—I know, I'm an ass!"—the grand old man, the great man, across from me, breaking his rule, to celebrate my birthday, with white wine at lunch.

It was a day like this, a bright beauty, every view a promise that something wonderful could happen.

And here, on the next page:

Le Bistro Alexandre

I came here often in those Montreal years, to feel urbane in my "salad days." It's on Peel a few blocks up from what was then Dorchester Boulevard, and is now Boulevard René Lévesque.

One time, after I'd dropped off that letter, there was the phone call at the bar! "You should have stayed—we could have had lunch—can you come up now, or…?" And then a year or so later, I brought him here to the Bistro. He'd never been before, though it was so close to the office. Sitting on a banquette, French peasants on the mural behind me, blood pudding and a conversation on dark things. Pierre, the waiter, served us. He's been here seventeen years now. And I see that Pierre (the other Pierre) came here again, and again, because he's there now, standing with the chef in some photos on the wall.

I have no photographs.

Did it happen at all?

I *do* have one blurry photograph—but I think of these dancers in the third person—he is Twisting, in his own delight, and she has one hand and one toe reaching out as if to grab him, or trip him, and it is in that one moment that I recognize *us*…

"I think of these dancers in the third person"

The Shoes

It was November 1st, 1985.

I didn't have anything remotely formal to wear.

The National Theatre School in Montreal was celebrating its 25th anniversary with a Gala Dinner and Dance. It was a pricey fundraiser, so unless they could part with a month's worth of rent, none of my schoolmates could attend. But as the recently elected Student Representative on the Board, I was invited. Martha Henry, from the first graduating class, was going to be there; Maureen Forrester, Marc Lalonde, Prime Minister Mulroney's Culture Minister, Marcel Masse—maybe two hundred people altogether; and amongst them all, a year and a half after his walk in the snow, the Right Honourable Pierre Elliott Trudeau.

Despite years of coaxing and cajoling from my family to awaken in me some sort of feminine approach to my attire, an interest in fashion never took. I certainly didn't decide to become an actor out of any sense of flamboyance—in fact, somewhere down there, maybe I became an actor because it meant somebody else would dress me....

So, after the school day ended, I went with a gang from class to Shannon Lawson's apartment to borrow a dress. We stopped in at a local dépanneur to buy Cheezies and beer and five-dollar wine, and carried it all in plastic bags to Shannon's. Everyone crowded around the closet, beer in hand, picking outfits for me to try on. Shannon was in her third and final year, and had a wild collection of dresses: exotic creatures that she'd bagged on various retro-shop safaris. And she knew things about accessorizing. The chosen dress was black, had a low-cut back and a long flared skirt and was simple and classic, and it didn't need *any* accessories, except stockings, which I had, and shoes, which I hadn't. I had a pair of Reeboks, a pair of snow-boots, and a pair of teeny-tiny feet, size six and a half—size seven at best.

Shannon's black heels were a size nine, but it was already getting dark, no time to go hunting around in anyone else's closet, and so I put them into one of the plastic bags from the dépanneur, and bounded back to the school in my dress and snow-boots. I slipped in the back door, with the sounds of the beginning gala echoing in the stairwell.

Downstairs in the locker room, I kicked off the boots and stepped into Shannon's dressy black heels. They hung like snowshoes on my little stocking feet.

I shuffled into the bathroom, stepped out of the shoes, and stuffed toilet paper into the toes; then I slapped them back on and *trolled* them upstairs.

The foyer of the school is quite grand, very tall ceilings, several pillars, and polished stone floors. I teetered near one of the pillars, and talked with Perry, who taught Improvisation. In the large room off to my right was a buffet of hors d'oeuvres: oysters on the half-shell, massive hunks of cheese, shrimp perched atop an ice sculpture like tiny pink seals upon a floe. Several guests were in there sampling the food, some were already downstairs, and others hovered in the foyer, champagne in hand and an eye on the front door.

Now, whether it was because everyone anticipated

his arrival and the collective energy focused radiant beams upon him; or whether, as some have said, he carried with him his own magnetic electricity—the atmosphere changed as Pierre Trudeau entered the building.

I watched him, tuxedoed, take in the space. He was followed by a small entourage. I recognized a board member. Trudeau pointed to the detail atop one of the pillars, then circled around…and came straight at me.

I thought about escaping—striding casually into the buffet room—then I remembered *the shoes,* and—pivoted—instead, to meet him.

It was the board member who made the introductions.

"So," Trudeau said, "you're an actress?"

"I'm a student—well—*actress*—in my second year here—"

"And you've been elected to serve on the Board of Governors?"

"By acclamation…"

"Congratulations!"

"Well, I mean, nobody else ran. We've met before" I said, "in 1981…I was in high school at the time—I'd asked you for an autograph and when I gave you the card to sign, my pinky got caught in the handover. You signed the card, handed it back, and said, "I'll keep the finger", and you started to walk on with me attached to you."

"Ah, yes…I remember that—I thought we'd met before…. Will you save me a dance?"

And then he was off with his gang around the

corner and downstairs to the Gym, where the dinner tables were set up.

I scuttled into the buffet room, and downed a couple of oysters and "tiny pink seals." The room cleared fairly quickly to follow Trudeau, yet the buffet was brimming. My God, the food! If only I could squirrel some away—I wished I'd borrowed some kind of purse from Shannon, because the dress had no pockets.

Downstairs I saw Martha Henry. I wanted to meet her but she was surrounded. I looked for my place card. Each guest had been assigned a seat at one of the scores of large round tables arranged for the dinner, at least six to a table. I had been placed with four strangers and a high-powered Montreal lawyer who was a Governor on the board. As soon as I sat down, I let the shoes fall from my feet.

I was three when Pierre Trudeau was elected to the House of Commons, four or five when Pearson appointed him Parliamentary Secretary. Mom and Dad went to Expo '67, and Dawn, our aptly named babysitter, stayed with my older sister and me, and taught us how to blow bubble gum. Trudeau was Parliamentary Secretary for about a year before Pearson made him Justice Minister—and right away he tabled the legislation to get the State out of our bedrooms, relaxing the laws on abortion, divorce and what was called "homosexual practices" in one fell swoop. It was about that time that *I* swooped headfirst down the staircase on my stuffed bear "Jingles", and got a sliver in my tongue from the hardwood floor.

Sometime during the chicken course, I glanced across the room to see who was where. Trudeau was seated near the corner of the gym, there were maybe five tables spaced out between us. He looked at me. I smiled, returned my attention to the whipped potato, and pretended to resume a fascinating conversation with the lawyer, who was looking the other way.

Later, as coffee and dessert were served I looked to the corner again. Trudeau turned at the same time, saw me, and rolled his eyes. Moments later I felt a hand on the back of my chair, "You won't forget my dance…?"

I tried to feel for the shoes that I'd dropped under the table, but I must have kicked them out of reach, so staying seated, I said, "Oh, are you leaving soon?"

"Well, how can I leave without having my dance?" And then he moved on.

Our television was in the living room, at 29 Hambly Avenue in Toronto, black and white, of course—but I remember my shows in colour, Mom and Dad's in black and white…*Mr. Dressup, Chez Hélène*: colour; news of The Official Languages Act: black and white. And certain television images are imprinted on my brain—not because I could comprehend them, but because they were linked with expressions I had never before seen on the faces of my parents: fear, shock, stunned outrage. They were transfixed by the French newsreader reading the manifesto; footage of the trunk of a car in a parking lot in the dark, and the Prime Minister's grim, grey face talking about the "law of the jungle". They were somehow as mesmerized by the Nightly News as I had been by Friendly Giant's little chairs or "Rusty the Rooster"—why, why, *why* is he in that bag?"

I spotted the errant shoes, stretched my legs to retrieve them and slipped them onto my feet. I moved to the centre of the gym and talked absently to some students who were acting as servers—

"but I remember my shows in colour"

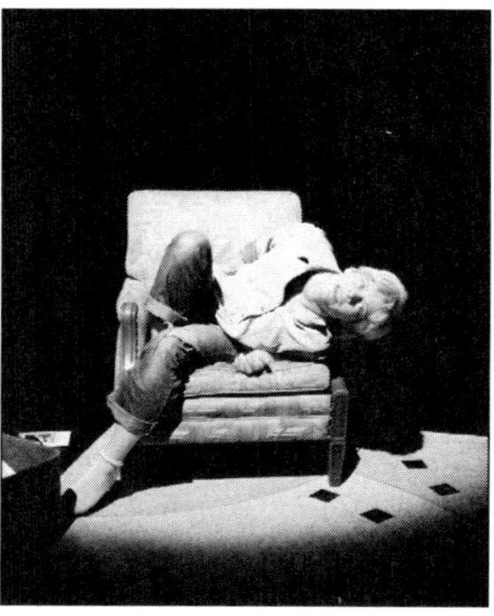

"Trudeau was talking to you!"

"I know, I know!"

"Trudeau ta parlait!"

"Oui, je sais…!"

I tried to regain composure. I tried to readjust the toilet paper in my shoes simply by wriggling my toes. It wasn't working, there was a gaping void under my left big toe, and a wad crumpled up under the baby-toe. I thought, This is RIDICULOUS, maybe if I can get to the ladies room, I can get *fresh* toilet paper and restore the stuffing. So, I maneuvered out of the gym to shuffle past the studio where the dancing was. Trudeau was standing there, hands clasped in front. He reached for my arm, "Now can we dance?" and he led me onto the dance floor.

The first song was a fast one. The toilet paper won't be enough to keep the boats on my feet! After the first spin, I grabbed hold of his hand and said, over the music:

"You know, I have TOILET PAPER in my SHOES—because (well) they're NOT MY shoes—they're too BIG...you see, and so this fast dancing is kind of tricky!"

He laughed, and stopped dancing. I thought of Voice Class and reminded myself to breathe.

We stood there instead and talked on the dance floor, but closely because of the music. He wanted to know how school was going, what I'd done in first year. I said, "It's been mostly great, very demanding; I've done a bit of O'Casey, took a stab at Cordelia—you know, this and that."

The next song started,

"Is this alright? For your *shoes*?"

We began a slow dance. His skin was finely freckled. (I had no idea how freckled he was). I was reminded of how the dress was open down to the middle of my back. As we danced, he talked about King Lear howling as he carried Cordelia; he wasn't familiar with *Juno and the Paycock,* though he knew of Sean O'Casey, he was mostly a fan of Racine and Corneille.

Trudeau thought that "The Theatre" was magnificent.

He wondered if I'd be free for lunch sometime.

"Well, they keep us hopping here. I suppose you could drop by the Cafeteria, and we could grab a grilled cheese. Right now, we're doing scenes from Chekhov with a Russian director; shortly we'll start a study of the Restoration Period. It's more than just research, we're supposed to *resuscitate the era*—scenes from thirteen plays to learn, dances, bawdy tavern songs in five part harmony, funeral music for Queen Mary—and sword-and-dagger and cloak-and-dagger fights—I'll be playing Lady Sneerwell, Mrs. Squeamish, Isabella, Lady Gay Spanker—"

He said, "Well, how about dinner?"

"Dollar-fifty Tuesdays," I said, "All-you-can-eat poutine at the Laurier Brasserie?"

Trudeau sort of tilted his head back, and studied me.

"Well, perhaps sometime, when you're not so busy—we could, I don't know, maybe go for a walk in the country?"

I said, "Hah-hah-heh-heh-Hah!" and I went back to the Restoration.

Not long after, my elegant and surprisingly shy partner was gone. I stood alone on the dance floor—dancers swirling around me—and I wondered about his invitations, wondered about my responses, then made my way out of the studio. I pulled off the black pumps, hitched up my dress, and started up the stairs in my stocking-feet, slipping and sliding down the terrazzo halls, hoping to catch him before he was out the door.

In the foyer two large men in coats watched me slide towards him.

"Yes—" Trudeau said as he turned, as if my arrival in this manner was the most natural thing in the world, "I should get your phone number—or, you can take mine…?"

"I'll take yours."

He gave me a piece of paper with his office number on it, saying he'd be in South Africa for a couple of weeks but that I could get in touch after that…*if* I wanted.

Trudeau took one of the shoes out of my grasp,

"Let me see..."

Reaching into the toe, he pulled out the wad of toilet paper. "I wasn't sure...I thought maybe you were teasing..." And then he carefully refitted the toilet paper, handed back the shoe, and then he was out the door.

A week later, knowing that he'd still be away, I dialed the office number.

"Heenan, Blaikie, Bonjour?"

"Bonjour. Je voudrais laisser une message pour Monsieur Trudeau?"

"Yes, what is the message?"

I gave my name and phone number and said,

"Could you leave this message—would you write: "Regarding...your invitation..."

"Yes...?!"

"...of a walk...in the country..?"

"Yes...?"

"Which country?"

The Long Black Car

A week after that, a long black car idled outside of my basement apartment; two large men in the front seat, wearing dark coats.

Pierre Trudeau stood behind me as I fumbled to lock my door. He took my arm as we crunched over the snow piled high against the curb and ducked into the back seat. The car moved silently towards Laurier.

"Would you like to go down to the Old Port?"

"That'd be great. I'd love to."

"We could go for dinner if you'd like, or just go for a walk?"

I had only borrowed a sweater this time, to wear with my jeans, and envisioned being barred from the kind of restaurant he might take me to.

"I've already eaten."

"Well, so have I, but I thought, if you were hungry…?"

"Not really, but thanks."

The car turned onto St. Denis, traveling south.

"I'm sorry it's so late. I was having dinner with John Turner—it was an arrangement we'd made a while ago, and I couldn't get out of it."

It wasn't immediately apparent what I should say to that. I said, "Oh…*how's* he?"

"He's fine, I think. I'll tell him you asked."

"I feel funny that you left your dinner early…"

"Well, I can see *him* anytime. *You're* harder to pin down."

The car crossed Notre Dame and headed down into the heart of Old Montreal.

"Shall we get out here?"

We stopped near Bonsecours, and the large fellow in the passenger seat opened the door for us. We walked west along St. Paul. The street was deserted except for us: the man in the long wool coat and beaver hat, the girl in the red ski-jacket and snow boots—and the long black car creeping a half a block behind.

"Are they Mounties?"

"Yes. They were assigned to 'watch out' for me when I left office. It's required I'm afraid. Not for much longer, thankfully. I think it's two years for the two of them, and then there'll just be one guy for a while after that."

He did a little hop and a skip and then slid along a sheer patch of ice covering the sidewalk.

"Wheee!" (He actually said that!) "Wheeeeee!"

So I slid too, and we skated for a block on our boots.

"Would you like to go in somewhere for a drink?" he asked, easing to a stop.

"Sure!"

Our breath steamed and danced between us. Up ahead on the other side of the street was a glowing stained-glass sign.

"Do you know that place?"

"I don't get down here much…we can give it a try…?"

As we got closer to the bar, I recognized it—from its counterpart in Toronto—as "Brandy's": a slightly plush pick-up joint. I considered suggesting we find another place, but he'd already opened the door. We stepped up and into a predominantly red barroom, with wing-back chairs and too many Tiffany-style lamps, and a long wooden bar propping up a horde of young, male students.

Pick-up joint or not, my companion was immediately surrounded.

"Mr. Trudeau!" "Mr. Trudeau!" "I'm in second year law, Mr. Trudeau!" "Well, all of us are." "We've just finished our first term papers!"

"So, you got them in on time?"

Whoooo!!

"Where, McGill?"

"Yeah!! Whoooo!!Mr. Trudeau!! Whoooo!! Mr. Trudeau!!!"

I had to step back as they crowded around him.

He chatted with them, grilled them, asking their views on apartheid and whether they thought the embargo against South Africa was a good idea.

I took off my parka, and hung it over the wing of a chair. The bright red jacket clashed against the scarlet upholstery. Beside the table, and set into the wall was a large aquarium, filled with an assortment of exotic fishes, and two small sharks.

"They're very bright," Trudeau said, as he joined me at the table.

"I'd forgotten that you've just come back from South Africa. Were you on holiday?"

"No…every so often there's a meeting of former Heads of State. This one was held in Johannesburg."

"But you weren't a Head of State, were you? I thought that job belonged to the Queen?"

"Well, you're right…but, as the Queen couldn't make it—"

"—they let you fill in."

"I guess I'm considered a former Head of State in this context, outside of the Commonwealth—I suppose it's simpler that way."

The waiter hovered.

"What will you have?" ***(Asked Trudeau)***, "Wine, beer, brandy, something to eat, something to drink?"

"A beer, I guess."

"Two beers."

The waiter ran through the list.

"I'll have a Tuborg, please."

"Two Tuborg."

"So, what do you meet about, you former Heads of State?"

"Oh, we talk about current issues in the world, a variety of things, and try to come up with solutions." He looked down at the edge of the table as he spoke, and down to the paisley pattern on the carpet.

"And then?"

"And then we hope we can make recommendations to whoever will listen."

"That's kind of comforting, that you get together that way—to talk—I mean, outside the pressures of the political—the political…*hullabaloo…*"

"Well, it's interesting. I hope we accomplish some things. It's always nice to travel."

"Is there any place you haven't been?"

"No—I think I've been to every country at one time or another, except Albania, of course."

"Maybe *that's* where we should go for our walk…?"

"Perhaps…*some* day."

"Do you plan to ever go?"

"It's not up to me; it's up to the Regime. Hey, you're asking all the questions! I want to know about Chekhov."

As I spoke about rehearsals his eyes lit up. I told him I was playing Olga in *The Three Sisters*.

"*The Three Sisters*!…Remind me, which one is Olga?"

"She's the eldest. She's the one who wants to get married."

"And is this a presentation that I can see?"

"No," I said, reaching for my glass, "It's more just an in-class exploration."

"Oh, that's too bad…maybe I can see the next one?"

"Maybe..." I took a gulp of beer.

"So, Olga...you want to get married...?"

I stifled a laugh and the beer threatened to go up my nose.

We talked some more about Olga and then about art and somehow got onto architecture...

"You should see the house. It was designed by Ernest Cormier. We could go up there now and have a tour before the guys take you home?"

Journey to Pine Avenue

From the street it looks like a *small* building, blocks of stone with eight horizontal panes of smoked glass and a large wooden door with a narrow window set into it near the top. Sometimes when I visit I will see an eye peering out and the crown of Pierre's head. I suspect that he is on tip-toe.

This house is not small at all. It sits at the base of the Mount Royal Park, and descends four floors.

In the entrance, four pairs of shoes sit by the right hand wall. Through the inner door, the first impression is of a Marble Sanctum. A polished stone floor is inlaid with marble squares in circles and overlapping rings. Cormier had laid the floor himself, but didn't quite get it finished. At the far end of the hall is a marble staircase with a brushed steel banister swooping up and around. But before you reach that, you find the kitchen on the left.

If it is evening, breakfast bowls are set for the boys on the counter, on three placemats with cartoon animal faces. Above is a shelf of political memorabilia: coffee mugs and beer steins with cartoon *Trudeau* faces.

Across the hall, smooth, black marble pillars stand on either side of the entrance to the atelier. In here, with all the windows, it feels like a kind of atrium: the ceiling starts at maybe eighteen feet, and lifts up to say, thirty feet, maybe even more. A black marble fireplace is against one wall and by it, a large Ming urn given to Trudeau by Mao Tse Tung.

The walls are covered with birch paper. Not birch bark, but a paper made from tiny delicate strips of blond wood, laid in such away as to create broad horizontal stripes because of the direction of the grain and the way the patterned strips catch the light.

This space has two areas for sitting. This first evening, we sit in the end nearest the park. It's on the right as you pass between the pillars and contains a long couch and four heavy Art Deco chairs. *Everything* is Art Deco, and everything was created by Ernest Cormier, including the massive hexagonal coffee table that sits on its own swivel amidst the chairs. On this table is a book of prints by M.C. Escher.

An upright piano stands against the wall, on it are photographs of Justin, Sacha and Michel—the only reminders of the boys in this grand space. Their space, the real living space, along with the swimming pool and sauna, is on the floors below.

So, after the tour, we pad in our socks to the liquor cabinet. Deng Xiao Ping (or Zhao Zhyiang?) had given Pierre a bottle of Moutai as a gift, but he didn't care for it. It was there amongst the cognacs, and I'd never tried it, so he poured me a small glass. We sat in adjacent chairs by the swiveling table, and I leafed through the Escher book. Escher's world is highly controlled and ordered, everything at right angles—but then he twists perception with another world within that structure, a world that seems *possible* and *impossible* at the same time…

Pierre asked me question upon question.

I told him that we'd moved from Toronto to the country when I was nine, how I'd built a cabin—Dad cut the logs to size, I trimmed the branches with an axe and set the logs upright into a trench and lashed them together like the boys did in *Lost in the Barrens*.

I told him about canoe camp when I was thirteen—paddling two hundred and fifty miles from Temagami to Timmins, and how on the first portage, carrying a sixty-pound pack, I sat on a log to catch my breath and was stung by wasps, (one sting for every year of my life) because I couldn't get the straps off to run clear, and how that trip was the most exhilarating adventure of my young life and when I got home I refused to sleep indoors for days.

I told Pierre how trees were part of my life—my dad is a landscape architect and Mom the daughter of a lumberman—"my family might make for a good Escher print: one side planting trees, the other cutting them down."

He asked how I came upon my interest in the theatre. I told him about Grampa, Dad's dad, who'd always written songs and poems and stuff for the stage—not quite plays—extended sketches and five act operettas that finished in ten minutes.

"He's also an inventor. He had a tree nursery in Cataraqui, Ontario, and invented *Scent-Off! Dog and Cat Repellent* to discourage neighbouring pets from peeing on your shrubs.

Scent Off! The slogan was: "It sends them *Elsewhere!*"

Pierre asked what kind of music I liked, and I said I was raised with jazz—Oscar Peterson, Errol Garner, Duke Ellington and Satchmo, Wild Bill Davidson and Buzzy Drootin; and on Sunday mornings, opera with pancakes. I think I might have told him my whole life story, a bit in awe of how much talking I was doing.

The Moutai was strange and intoxicating. I couldn't manage more than a couple of polite sips... ***(Swooning as if into a faint...Pause.)*** Nah!—that part never happened...

I think it was about midnight when I said goodnight and again, the long black car was waiting to take me back to my apartment.

Escher's Staircase
(Finding a draft of a letter)

Dear Pierre:

Since Friday evening, I have been stumbling around on Escher's staircase, not sure whether I am going up or down, and having no idea how to get off the damn thing. Perhaps I am making a mountain out of a molehill—but I had to write this to give my conscience a rest. I had a wonderful time with you on Friday. I don't for a moment regret going out with you, but I know I can't become romantically involved, and I have been kicking myself for not having had the courage to say so.

It's presumptuous of me to assume you would be interested in me in that way; but on the other hand, it may seem naïve of me to think you would be interested in me in any other *way.*

I feel very silly writing this, and just hope you will put yourself in my shoes, toilet paper and all. You are Pierre Trudeau *(and you do have a bit of a reputation) and I am Miss X, or Miss Y… Still I'd hate to think I lost a friend because I was too hasty in drawing the lines.*

Here I am, you see, going three steps up this staircase and at the same time I am back where I started. I only hope you might offer me some sort of ladder so that I can climb down from this contraption; and that you might forgive my idiocy.

Yours,

Brooke

P.S. I have the day off, and may summon the courage to call you.

The letter was dropped off at Heenan Blaikie. I gave it to one of the receptionists and then took off. I wandered around downtown, mustering that courage. Who am I? Who the heck do I think I am?

I went into a place I liked, Le Bistro Alexandre. I sat at the bar and ordered a soup and a ginger ale. I asked the bartender if there was a phone, and he brought me the bar phone.

"Heenan, Blaikie, bonjour…?"

"Bonjour…uh…est-ce que je peut parler avec Monsieur Trudeau?"

"One moment, and I'll put you through to his secretary."

"Le Bureau de Monsieur Trud*eau*, Mister *Tru*deau's office?"

I said my name and started to explain that I'd dropped off a letter—

"Oh, yes Brooke! You know it's funny, *my* name is *Mrs.* Brooke!"

"Is it spelled with an 'e'?"

"Yes, with an 'e'! Now, Mr. Trudeau is in a meeting, but give me your number, I know that he wants to speak with you."

So I gave her the Bistro's number from a book of matches on the bar.

While I nursed my soup, the phone rang twice; the bartender answered in French, spoke briefly and then hung up. Ten minutes later, BRRing! he brought me the phone.

"Oh, Brooke! This is Mrs. Brooke! Brooke, I have Mr. Trudeau on the line."

How strange to sit at a bar, peeling the layers of a cardboard coaster and hearing *that voice* in my ear:

"You should've stayed when you dropped off the letter—we could've had lunch together! Can you come up now, or are you busy? We can at least talk for a bit…?"

He was so…he was very…***(Finding passage in a journal.)***

I find him very shy, very introspective—yet he thinks out loud, and was wearing a plaid suit and a striped tie. He quoted, by heart, my letter as he spoke, and said that writing letters is a lost art. He said he wasn't looking for a romantic relationship either. He was content with his life. He had thought about me over the weekend and even though we were "both loners" he enjoyed my company and it shouldn't matter if we had lunch or went to a movie once in a while.

Looking back now, I see it *was* a Romance, in a *Boy's Own* kind of way: we hiked up the trails on Mount Royal in January, dodging the cross-country skiers, and we slid—one hand on the rail—down the ice-covered east side staircase; we traveled north in the summer to his lake house, stopping for gas and donuts alongside cars with deer carcasses strapped to the roof and hood! We paddled in the rain, hiked, swam, set two beaver traps and had peanut butter on toast while waiting for guests to arrive. Then we all went for another hike and then we had lasagna.

We never held hands, except to give or take a lift out of the water or up a steep slope; never lied down together, except in the sauna…. At no time, since the dance, did Pierre approach me with anything resembling seduction.

"I have a beaver problem," he said.

This was when we were paddling in the rain. We glided to one edge of the lake, where a large stand of trees had been swamped, and pulling the canoe up, we hiked to the first small dam.

"Pierre, remember the *Scent-Off! Dog and Cat Repellent*? Well, apparently the New Brunswick government has a beaver problem too and asked Grampa to send a stronger version of *Scent-Off!*

Grampa calls it *B-Vair!*"

So Pierre ordered a box of beaver repellent.

Dark Night
(Reading from another passage in the journal)

November 2nd, 1986.

For the first time I've found a character that I really wanted to play, 'Anna Petrovna Voynitzeva', but I've been cast as 'Sasha'. Bore me to tears!

It seems as though I've lived several different lives, and I'm not particularly pleased with how I'm handling the present one. I don't mean that in a metaphysical sense. I mean that horse, dogs, cabin, canoeing—constituted one life; working backstage in New York and Ireland, traveling alone in Europe, another; working in Toronto in the law firm, another.

I don't think, now, that I'm…

It's above and beyond the…the day to day…

…Pierre called back on Friday. Haven't spent any time with him since July.

I want to talk with him about Russia and also about the leadership.

I want to talk about wanderlust and about wanting to do something of consequence!

He's all booked up—lunch with an old friend today, then giving a send-off for Mayor Drapeau; Jacques Hébert is coming in from Ottawa, etc., etc., etc. So, instead, I'm dropping over to the house Wednesday evening after rehearsal. I feel estranged—as though I need to make a new impression. I want to be of value, but I have no idea how...Maybe in observations about being human—human stuff.

I wonder if he has ever yearned for something without knowing what it was. I could show him the feeling: Take a sip of cognac, think of a poem. As you're thinking, swirl it in your mouth, take a tiny breath, and slowly swallow. That burning all through you—is like yearning.

I think I should promise myself one thing. In view of the fact that I need to reestablish the friendship and want to be of value, I will talk about longing and tell him a poem.

I thought about the promise I had made, but there was no place for it.

I arrived at the house around nine that Wednesday evening. Pierre was watching for me through the window. He didn't want the boys to hear the doorbell and want to come up. I removed my boots and he put my coat in the closet. Was there anything I wanted? I asked for a cognac. He poured a tiny splash of Martell into a snifter for himself and a large portion of Rémy for me.

The house was dark, except for the glow of an exterior light shining through the southern window.

Pierre sat in a small armchair in front of the window. I sat facing him. On either side of the window are two huge stone friezes of an Ancient Greek thumbing his nose at a pursuer.

I started to feel as though I'd done something wrong. He just sat there.

"How was your trip to Russia?"

"Russia...is Russia."

"I'm having a hard time at school lately. I'm not…I can't…

Pause.

You know, I thought at eighteen that I can't possibly live to twenty-five—that I shouldn't expect it because I've experienced so many fascinating things, and had so many moments of ecstasy—how can there possibly be more?"

"Yes…well…you'll likely live a while longer."

"What I'm being challenged with isn't interesting me these days—I'm not sure acting is right for me, or if I'm right for it—I'm sorry, I'm not being very articulate…did *you* have trouble at school?"

"Well, much of it was interesting, and the rest: well…I applied myself."

Pause.

"Hey—How did the wildflower grass-seed take, up at the lake?"

"It's *remarkable* how *city* kids are always amazed at how things grow in the country."

That wasn't fair! But I was too surprised to fire back. He sighed.

"You're probably tired, I should go."

"No, I'm not *'tired'*—it's just that last week I was out a lot…and I needed this week to catch up on my rest."

I can't say if he ever looked at me—certainly not when I was looking at him. I finished my cognac in a searing gulp,

"It's 10 o'clock, I should go, I've got rehearsal tomorrow."

He walked me to the closet to fetch my coat. He helped me on with it, as always careful to lift my long hair free of the collar, and then he wrapped his arms around me and whispered in my ear,

"Lost souls…."

And he didn't let go for the longest time.

Tut-tut

"A friend said once—and I'll be sworne,
'Twas all well taken—
There is a way, a means, he said, for Friends to talk, and that is to be intimate:
To share the kind of close rapport, to lift the mask we show to most.
But heare me now, th'other night—I could not tell—
Was that the mask or he?
It is as much as I can do to keep the terms of this precise;
I had myself lost much that night—so many things, I had not said
And all the old desires to naught,
And now with him not quite at hand, I fear the loss of Friendship.
Contain it? Well I know not how:
It hangs in the air like smoke—and even now the icy wind
Upon some wayward course it blows.
For in these times he stands at distance,
His silences, and sighs, and now I know not what have left me
Lost.
And what is there that I can do, to prove a worthy friend to him?
I ask myself this question much, but yet have found no answer.
O Reason, mind, and patience—Can I let all this slip away sans mot?
Tut, tut: it is the heart, dear friend, 'tis here, 'Tis Heere."

Oh, the torments of mailing a letter like that!

A few days later, he phoned and we met for coffee.

"I was amazed that you were able, just like that, to find such an appropriate passage in Shakespeare. Which play is it?"

"It's not actually from a play—it's a mish-mash of bits of Shakespeare rearranged—-and me faking him."

"People always think of me as a reader, that I know all the great writers and have studied them all — but that's not really true."

"What about your essays with the quotes under the titles, from Thomas Aquinas and de Tocqueville—what about them?"

"Well, I've read snatches here and there, and found by chance passages which pertained to my beliefs, but I didn't read their *Works*...So much of my reading time for so long has been restricted to bills and briefs and other legal documents...and I'm a slow reader."

I pulled out a book I had bought for him, a paperback copy like mine, of Yeats' *Selected Poetry*. He seemed overwhelmed that it was a gift.

"When you are old and grey and full of sleep,
And nodding by the fire, take down this book,
And slowly read and dream of the soft look
Your eyes had once, and of their shadows deep;"

As I read the poem the smile melted from his lips and he stared down at his hands, "You're going to make me cry..." and his eyes were watery.

He took the book from my hands and found another poem,

"'The Second Coming'…read this one, will you?"

I got as far as "Spiritus Mund-EYE", and he said, "I think it's "MunDEE", and I said, "Well, *you* should read it!"

Which he did, in his growly half-whisper:

"Turning and turning in the widening gyre,
The falcon cannot hear the falconer;
Things fall apart; the centre cannot hold;
Mere anarchy is loosed upon the world…"

And then Pierre spoke of the dark night at the house,

"You know, my old great friends, Pelletier and Hébert, and maybe one or two others, have known me long enough to recognize when I am 'in my shell'… Perhaps in a few years you will recognize it too—although I think you already have a handle on it."

I walked with him to the corner. A lady in some sort of striped fur stopped him to say "Hiiii!!" and as she walked on, Pierre turned and sighed,

"That's my life…"

Birthday Lunch

My life was changing. It was June 1st, 1987.

School was finished. I was leaving shortly for Toronto to play Miranda in *The Tempest*.

I was more together than usual, wearing a skirt.

"Where are the torn jeans? My goodness, you *look* like a *girl*!"

Pierre pointed out his window to the rooftop of the Hôtel de la Montagne,

"There's a restaurant up there, would that suit you…?"

He carried a plastic bag with him, and was very chipper on the walk over, but he was limping a bit.

"No it's fine; I damaged the cartilage in my knee while running on uneven ground. The doctors have said I might need a simple operation."

People smiled at him as usual, but with a glint of complicity, several giving him the 'thumbs up': gestures in response to his recent attack on the Prime Minister and the Meech Lake Premiers. He'd written that Mulroney was a "weakling," and they were "a bunch of snivelers throwing tantrums."

He asked what I did for my birthday, and as we walked along he squeezed my shoulders in "Congratulations for *making it to twenty-five!*"

We stopped in at Sports Experts. He had to return a part from the stationary bicycle he was using as part of his physiotherapy. While there he grabbed a pair of shorts and slipped into the change booth. He emerged in his shirt and tie, brown socks and shoes, with the shorts on—stiff and baggy,

"What do you think? I guess the material will relax, won't it, after I've worn them a few times?"

Then we went to Birks. Birks had the wedding registry for a senator-friend's daughter. The saleslady pulled a lunch setting from the glass case and said it was $450.00.

"Wow", would that be for six people or for twelve?"

"No, Mr. Trudeau, that is the price of a single setting. A single setting has been a popular choice."

Pierre chose a gravy ladle, for $165.00.

"What do you think? *(He asked me.)* Would this be a good choice?"

What do you think? What do *you* think? You! What do *you* think? Always questioning, always checking, always engaging.

When we got to the rooftop and sat down, he ordered a half bottle of white wine, dug into the plastic bag and pulled out a tiny book of Shakespeare's sonnets. Inside is written, *Pierre Elliott, 1968.*

"Somebody gave it to me on my first Christmas as Prime Minister. I wrote an inscription in it, so no one would think you'd stolen it..."

For Brooke for her birthday—
and the best of memories
Pierre E.T. 1987

Letters

(Reading from the pages that were folded into the sonnet book.)

Dear Pierre,

It has been a while since I've written you a letter.

There is a café on Bloor Street, near my home, where I like to have coffee and write. I am here now, with assorted sheaves of paper, procrastinating.

That's not to say that writing to you is a dalliance, but it is a much enjoyed diversion—I'm supposed to write and perform a monologue for an Amnesty International Benefit. One way or another, I can't seem to come up with much, and it happened that my thinking of human rights led my mind to you.

So here I am. Procrastinating.

I wonder if this has been sitting on your desk, awaiting your return from some faraway land. Happy Birthday! Maybe you'd like a book of Canadian poetry, inscribed "With Fond Memories" but I should like to sign it Ingrid Bergman or something, so it would carry special weight.

Work, now, consists mainly of auditioning. Tomorrow I have an audition for *The Muppet Show*, as a Muppeteer! And I'm still waiting to hear about a film I auditioned for last month, set in the mining district of Cobalt, Ontario. Sometimes it takes a long time before you hear that you didn't get a role. And sometimes it gets me down, especially on rent day—to discover what it means to be earning well below the poverty line. But it is my choice, and when I am working I love the challenges.

I think, since I've been involved in this profession, I've become more of a Canadian. I used to think that this was a dull country, with no history, that nothing of universal significance can come of a people who haven't been united in a cause—but little struggles and personal conflicts are universal……because our basic needs are in common: love, desire, the need to be understood, the need to be counted.

It bothers me that the arts are so insignificant in the eyes of this government— Yet when something glorious is born, a great Canadian play or film—or ballet, people are proud, even though they don't go to see it. But as history and human frailty would have it, nothing of consequence is ever truly appreciated until it's gone and put into some sort of historical context. It is both exciting and frustrating to be amongst people who are trying to create.

I wonder if this Free Trade deal might be a turning point—I don't know much about it, the government seems determined to keep us uninformed, but it sure smells like wet socks…one possible good thing might be that we are forced to ponder what this country means to us, what we want to "stand on guard" for, and that we may have to fight for it. In doing so, maybe we'd collectively discover that we do have a Culture!

Ah, I must stop this now, and get back to human rights.

Much love,

Brooke

Dear Brooke,

You will know by now that I am not much of a letter writer... But your own letter correctly assumed that it would only be read after I had returned "from some faraway land." In fact, I was away for most of October, trekking in Kashmir and Bhutan...

What a joy to be awaited by your letter, your wise thoughts on Canada and the trade deal, and the excitement and frustration arising from your profession.

I am sure Ingrid Bergman would never have been such a friend...

By now your monologue for Amnesty will have been delivered; I would like to hear it from you sometime, or failing that, to read it. I feel you must have made it soar.

As for me, I am busy co-editing a book of essays on the Just Society. That should keep me busy until winter skiing comes along.

I send you all good thoughts in friendship, and a big hug,

Pierre

Dear Brooke,

Thank you for sending the delightful children's book you wrote—*zubba-zubba-zubba-zubba...* ***(Skipping over bits while reading.)***

I hope you will not mind if I risk a mild criticism, since we both love poetry: the lines do not always scan as well as they should.

Essentially the poem is written in anapæstic tetrameters, each foot consisting of two short syllables followed by one long; and each verse being composed of four feet. Now of course you may throw in an iambus for effect (and he has marked the stresses in pencil on the page): "His Mother said, Lucas, there's something more." After all, Browning did it: "I jumped to the saddle and Joris and he"

But why do you finish the line with "There's something more", wherein the apostrophe "s" makes it impossible to scan, and when you might have written: "His mother said: Lucas there *is* something more."

Four lines later you repeat the same mistake and spoil what could have been a perfect anapæstic tetrameter.

That, by way of example, and there are many more I could give. But by now you will be dismissing me as a purist, which I suppose I am (when it comes to prosody). Perhaps I stumbled on E.A. Poe's *A Rationale of Verse* when I was too young…

Dear Pierre,

Thank you for the—*zubba-zubba-zubba-zubba…* ***(Skipping over bits.)***

…But since you sent me back to school, don't you think that the form might be logaoedic rather than anapaestic? Maybe it allows for excessive license, but logaoedic verse—a combination of iambs and anapests is an accepted form of prosody, used by Blake in *"Ah, Sunflower,"* Swinburne in *"Chorus,"* and Byron in *"The Destruction of the Sennacherib."*

Regardless, you can be sure I will keep the discussion in mind for the next attempt…

2 / .....

But why do you finish the line with "There's something more", wherein the apostrophy "s" makes it impossible to scan, and when you might have written

His Mother said: "Lucas, there is something more."

Four lines later you repeat the same mistake (apostrophy "s") and spoil what could have been a perfect anapaestic tetrameter:

And his Father sang, "Lucas, there is something more."

That, by way of example; and there are many more I could give. But by now you will be dismissing me as a Purist, which I suppose I am (when it comes to prosody). Perhaps I stumbled on E.A. Poe's "A Rationale of Verse", when I was too young!

Happy New Year to you and your family, and to David, and hopes that we will keep in touch.

As ever,

Last Letter

September, 21st, 2000

Dear Pierre,

There's a poem by Matthew Arnold, "Dover Beach," in which he expresses a yearning and a profound melancholia triggered by the sound of grating pebbles as the sea's waves toss them up the strand.

This past summer I lived near Diligent River, Nova Scotia, across from Cape Split. Tides in that region have been recorded at fifty-four feet. The play I was doing was *Of the Fields, Lately*, and it engendered a powerful response from the local audience. Often I couldn't sleep after the show, I'd sit on my porch, watch the sky turn and listen to the sea. Even in my bed I could hear, most nights, that same sound—and, most nights, I thought of you.

I have wanted to write to you for so long, but didn't know what to say. I still don't, but that sound from the shore and something too in the spirit of that landscape is with me still, and insists that I try.

I'm back in Toronto and I'm sitting by the water, and it's not the sea below me, but the lake is rough tonight and there's that same sound: "Begin, and cease, and then again begin…"

I kick myself for letting so much time slip by, for not maintaining contact with you, for not expressing myself, however inadequately, about the loss of your son, Michel.

Perhaps, as an actor, I've always assumed other people's words are better:

Jim Harrison—the American author—wrote, "We would like to think that the whole starry universe would curdle at such a monstrosity; the arms of the Southern Cross drooping, the constellation of Orion twisted askew…"

And maybe you remember a Yeats poem I once read to you:

"…how Love fled
And paced upon the mountains overhead
And hid his face amid a crowd of stars."

You are a treasure to me. We are an amalgam of people we have met along the way. And you —knowing you and having you as a friend has become a part of me. You have given me such exquisite memories and unique hope. You are a part of my imagination, a spark in my mind's eye, a spur to my confidence.

I would like to hop on the train and visit with you again. Maybe we can recite more Yeats; maybe I'll give you my rendition of Dover Beach?

You let me know when.

Until then, please take good care…

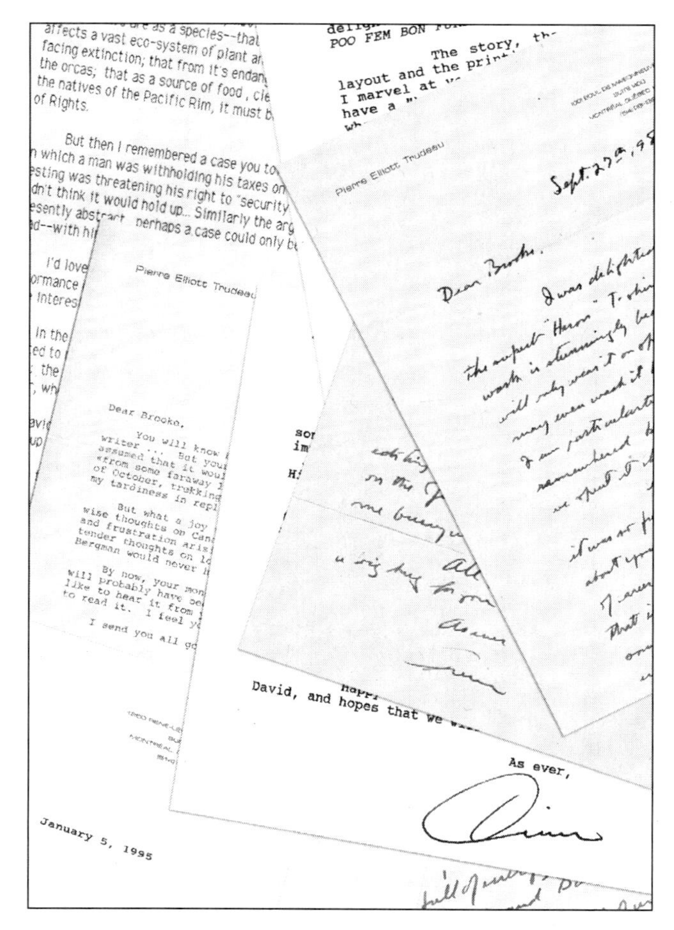

affects a vast eco-system of plant a
facing extinction; that from it's endan
the orcas; that as a source of food , cl
the natives of the Pacific Rim, it must
of Rights.
But then I remembered a case you to
n which a man was withholding his taxes on
esting was threatening his right to "security
dn't think it would hold up... Similarly the ar
esently abstract perhaps a case could only b
d--with hi
I'd love
ormance
Interes
In the
ed to
the
wh
avi
up
Pierre Elliott Trudeau
Dear Brooke,
You will know
writer ... But you
assumed that it wou
from some faraway
of October, trekkin
my tardiness in repl
But what a joy
wise thoughts on Can
and frustration aris
tender thoughts on lo
Bergman would never
By now, your mon
will probably have be
like to hear it from
to read it. I feel y
I send you all g
January 5, 1995
POO FEM BON
The story,
layout and the print
I marvel at
have a
Pierre Elliott Trudeau
Sept. 27
Dear Brooke.
I was delighted
the superb "Haro
work is stunningly be
will only wear it on
may even wash it
I am particularly
remembered
it was so
about you
That
David, and hopes that we
As ever,

The Long Black Car Revisited

Seven days after I sent that letter, throughout the next weekend and for most of the following week, Pierre's voice filled the airwaves, and the television and newspapers were saturated with images of Canadians—some crying, some clutching roses or photographs, farmers lining railway tracks, secretaries and C.E.O.s crowding the barricades together; thousands standing on Parliament Hill, shivering for hours in the autumn chill waiting to pay their respects.

"United in Grief" had been the headline in Saturday's *Globe*.

On the day of the funeral, amongst the crowds in front of Notre Dame, *I* didn't feel united, even with myself. I felt disembodied.

I'd been standing close to the street, the press corps paddock that lined the steps of the Basilica, was to my right. A middle-aged East Indian couple stood beside me. Between them they recited, in accented English, the names of almost everyone who passed on the roadway:

"Look, there's Iona Campagnola, and there's André Ouellette; and Ed Shreyer…and oh, that's—what's his name—it's on the tip of my tongue—ohh…!"

Another man leaned forward, "That's Ray Hnatyshyn," he said.

Strangers whispered to strangers, "I'll be able to tell my grandchildren I was here."

Fidel Castro had been the first to receive cheers as he stepped out of his car, and that had started the ball rolling.

Jimmy Carter, "Ooohhhhh!"

Joe Clark, "Huzzahhh!"

Some even cheered Mulroney. Or maybe it was Mila they were cheering, but then a voice behind me said, "Ooh, I wouldn't be caught dead in that."

Then it fell quiet, and a delicate clapping began, and was sustained, hand to hand, in a kind of ritualistic wave, from the first moment the Mounties came into view in their slow march behind the hearse, until the casket on their shoulders had disappeared into the open doors of the Basilica.

The shy applause of thousands of people.

I didn't want to go inside. I'd driven from Toronto to go, but now it didn't feel right, it felt awful.

I found an opening in the barricade and squeezed through it onto the street. There I truly was separated, walking along the empty boulevard while the throngs were hemmed in on either side, their focus now on the giant screen in front of Notre Dame.

I passed through another barrier at the corner and turned left.

It was as if a giant switch had been tripped. Not only did I find myself suddenly alone, but the sounds of the crowd and the broadcast had vanished, absorbed by the massive limestone buildings.

My footsteps echoed as I walked, in heels, past the Centaur Theatre and down to St. Paul. The cafés were open as I turned eastward, but they too were deserted. I could see a television through one window; saw the Archbishop, looking down.

Up ahead on the left was an open door. The stained-glass sign hanging above it said "Brandy's." I stepped inside. It was empty except for two men sitting on stools at the long bar. A large Canon camera sat on top of the bar, and one of the men was speaking quietly into a cell phone in a New York accent, his notepad open on his knee.

Though the volume was off, their eyes were on the television, on Jacques Hébert's sad, silent face.

I asked the bartender for a glass of cognac, and carried it to the back of the room. There, set into the back wall was the aquarium. I'd forgotten all about the aquarium! I wondered if they could be the same fish?

> ***At this point—a skating, traveling re-creation of that first outing:***
>
> ***Pierre behind me at the door, taking my arm over the snow, ducking into the back seat, "Oh how's he?"; and then out again, gesturing at the Mounties, hop skip, sliding on the frozen sidewalk, breath dancing, entering the excited barroom, "Mister Trudeau!", the boys, the fish, the fidgety feet... "So, Olga..." the laughing, the beer up my nose...***

The sound of pealing bells drifted in through the open door, signaling the end of the funeral. The two journalists who had been sitting at the bar were now standing in the doorway with the bartender.

I picked up my cognac and went to stand with them, and together we listened, as the bells rang out for ages, and echoed for ages, up and down the streets of stone.

Over the closing music two answering-machine messages can be heard:

Beep. "Brooke? Pierre Trudeau. Wondering if we can have lunch or drinks sometime. Let me know when you're in town—or Uptown... Downtown... Bye bye."...

Beep. "This is a message for Brooke. Tell her Pierre called and that she should 'break a leg' and that I'd like to find a time to come and see the play, so she can call me when she has a moment, at the office."

Lights fade.

The End.

Cape Split from Diligent River shore August 2000.

A List of References in *Trudeau Stories*
Compiled by Stephanie Baptist

There are a multitude of references in *Trudeau Stories*. Here they are under different categories, in order of appearance. Some of the more obscure or metaphoric references are explained below, others left for class research and exploration.

CANADIAN POLITICAL REFERENCES

The Right Honorable Pierre Elliott Trudeau
If you would like to learn more about Pierre Trudeau, Brooke Johnson recommends John English's two volume biography: *Citizen of the World: The Life of Pierre Elliott Trudeau Volume One: 1919-1968* and *Just Watch Me: The Life of Pierre Elliott Trudeau: 1968-2000*, published by Knopf Canada. Also, for a great taste of the social impact of Trudeau, she recommends Catherine Annau's award-winning documentary, *Just Watch Me: Trudeau and the 70's Generation*, NFB, 1999.

René Lévesque
Founder of the Parti Québécois and Premier of Québec from 1975 to 1986.

Marc Lalonde
Liberal politician and member of Trudeau's cabinet.

Brian Mulroney
Progressive Conservative. Prime Minister of Canada from 1984 to 1993.

Marcel Masse
Cabinet minister in Mulroney's government.

"His Walk in the Snow"
There have been mentions of other walks in the snow in Trudeau's political life, both metaphoric and actual, but this reference is the best known… On February 29, 1984 after judo with the boys, a "long walk in the snow", and a sauna, Pierre Trudeau decided to step down, ending his fifteen-year tenure as Prime Minister. He formally retired on June 30. (The time frame cited in

the play—"it had been a year and a half"—is a bit off to compensate for the difference between that snowy leap year night and the actual departure from the PMO.)

The House of Commons
The lower house of the Parliament of Canada, where the democratically elected Members of Parliament make speeches, put forth motions for debate (though debate is not always allowed by the government) and pass legislation on to the Senate for ratification into law.

Lester Pearson
Liberal. Prime Minister of Canada from 1963-1968.

"...The State Out of Our Bedrooms" (Bill C150)
In introducing this Bill, Trudeau paraphrased an expression borrowed from an editorial in the *Globe and Mail* newspaper by Martin O'Malley, dated 1967-Dec-12.

Before this legislation was passed, if you were were gay and sexually active and someone reported you, you could go to jail.

The Official Languages Act
This 1969 federal statute declares French and English to be the official languages of Canada.

"The Newsreader Reading the (FLQ) **Manifesto**;
`The Trunk of a Car in a Parking Lot in the Dark';
`The Law of the Jungle"
All of these references have to do with the October Crisis of 1970 when the FLQ (le Front de libération du Québec) committed terrorist acts in the name of Québec nationalism. "The Manifesto" was broadcast by CBC/Radio-Canada as part of the FLQ's demands. "The trunk of a car" is where Minister of Labour, Pierre Laporte, was found dead after being kidnapped by the FLQ. In a televised statement the day he invoked the War Measures Act, Trudeau said the government would not give in to "crude blackmail," by replacing the legal system with "the law of the jungle."

Mayor Jean Drapeau
Mayor of Montreal from the mid-1950s through the mid-80s.

Jacques Hébert
Gerard Pelletier
Long time journalist friends of Trudeau, Hébert served as a Senator from 1983-1998 and Pelletier was an MP for Hochelaga from 1965-1975.

"The Meech Lake Premiers"
This term refers to a 1987 meeting hosted by Brian Mulroney at Lac Meech, PQ, and attended by the ten provincial premiers to negotiate proposed amendments to the Constitution. Agreement was not reached and the Meech Lake Accord was not ratified.

Iona Campagnola
Andre Oulette
Liberal cabinet ministers.

Ed Shreyer
Ray Hnatyshyn
Former Governors-General of Canada.

Fidel Castro
Communist revolutionary who led Cuba from 1959 through 2008.

Jimmy Carter
President of the USA from 1976 through 1980.

Joe Clark
Progressive Conservative. Prime Minister of Canada 1979/80.

Mila Mulroney
Wife of Progressive Conservative Prime Minister Brian Mulroney.

MONTREAL REFERENCES

Hotel de la Montagne
One of the last family-owned hotels in Montreal. Closed in 2012.

Bistro Alexandre
Parisian-style bistro in Montreal, now called Chez Alexandre.

Dorchester Boulevard renamed René Lévesque
East-west artery in downtown Montreal.

Dépanneur
"Deps" are common in Montreal. They are small convenience stores that commonly sell wine and beer.

Laurier Brasserie
A tavern around the corner from the National Theatre School.

Heenan Blaikie (Deslaurier and Binnington)
The Montreal law firm where Trudeau worked after retiring from politics.

Laurier Ave
St. Denis Ave
Major Montreal streets. Laurier is named for Sir Wilfred Laurier, Prime Minister of Canada from 1896 to 1911. St. Denis is the street where the National Theatre School is located.

Brandy's
A bar in Old Montreal.

McGill
One of Canada's best and oldest universities.

Mount Royal Park
Two hundred hectare park on the mountain in Montreal.

Notre Dame Basilica
Gothic church in old Montreal that opened in 1830.

Centaur Theatre
Montreal's largest English-language theatre company.

POP CULTURE REFERENCES

Expo '67
The world's fair was held in Montreal from April through October 1967, during Canada's centennial year. It sparked renewed interest in Canadian identity.

***Mr. Dressup; Chez Hélene; The Friendly Giant* (and Rusty the Rooster)**
Canadian television shows for children during the 1960s and '70s. *Chez Hélene* was intended to teach rudimentary French to Anglophone children.

***Boy's Own* Magazine**
A magazine published from the early 1800s through the mid-1900s intended to entertain and build character in pre-teen boys.

The Muppet Show
A family television series created by puppeteer Jim Henson in the 1970s.

Ingrid Bergman
Swedish-born film actress and movie star in the mid-twentieth century.

"UNITED IN GRIEF had been the headline in Saturday's *Globe*"
Refers to an article written by Tu Thanh and Mark MacKinnon in the Saturday, September 30, 2000 *Globe and Mail*.

POETIC, LITERARY AND THEATRE REFERENCES

National Theatre School of Canada/Ecole National De Theatre du Canada
Canada's only co-lingual post-secondary institution dedicated to training theatre professionals.

Sean O'Casey (*Juno & The Paycock*)
Irish playwright, born in 1880.

***King Lear*, Cordelia**
Shakespearean tragedy. Cordelia is the youngest and favourite daughter of the title character.

Racine
Corneille
17th century French dramatists.

Anton Chekhov
19th century Russian playwright and short story writer.

Lady Sneerwell
Mrs. Squeamish
Lady Gay Spanker
Isabella
Characters from English plays: *School for Scandal* (Sheridan), *The Country Wife* (Wycherley), *London Assurance* (Boucicault), and *The Wonder: A Woman Keeps A Secret* (Centlivre).

Lost in the Barrens
A 1956 adventure story by Canadian author Farley Mowat.

Anna Petrovna Voynitzeva
A character in *Wild Honey*, an adaptation of Chekhov's *Platonov* by English playwright Michael Frayn.

William Butler Yeats
Irish poet, born 1865, died 1939.

Miranda in *The Tempest*
A principal character (the daughter of Prospero) in the Shakespeare's final play.

"I jumped to the saddle and Joris and he"
From a rollicking poem by Robert Browning (1812–89), "How they Brought the Good News from Ghent to Aix" Trudeau misremembers the word "sprang" as "jumped"in his letter; the poem starts:
"I sprang to the saddle, and Joris, and he;
I gallop'd, Dirck gallop'd, we gallop'd all three;"

Anapaestic, Iambic, Logaoedic; Tetrameter
These words describe poetic meter, which is the basic rhythmic structure of verse.

Edgar Allen Poe
A 19th century American author.

William Blake
Swinburne
Byron
Matthew Arnold
English poets.

Of the Fields, Lately
A Canadian classic by playwright David French, part of his Mercer family saga.

Jim Harrison
The quote is from Harrison's 1980 novella, *Legends of the Fall*.

OTHER POLITICAL–CULTURAL HISTORICAL REFERENCES

Nortel
Stock in this telecommunications company, Nortel Networks Corporation, crashed in 2002, putting 60,000 employees out of work and crippling the accounts of thousands of Canadian investors.

Embargo against South Africa
In the 1980s, countries opposed to South Africa's apartheid policies imposed an arms embargo, an oil embargo, and other sanctions on the country.

The Commonwealth
An international association consisting of the United Kingdom together with the previous colonies of the British Empire.

Ernest Cormier
Canadian engineer and architect born in 1885.

Art Deco
A visual style that flourished in the 1920s through the 1940s and is characterized by bold geometric shapes.

Moutai
China's best-known liquor, made with sorghum.

M.C. Escher
Dutch graphic artist born in 1898, known for his mathematically-inspired woodcuts and lithographs.

Ming Dynasty
Ruling dynasty of China for 276 years, from 1368–1644.

Mao Tse Tung
Also known as "Mao Zedong" or "Chairman Mao." Chinese Communist revolutionary and the founding father of the People's Republic of China, which he governed from its establishment in 1949 until his death in 1976.

Justin, Sacha (Alexandre) and Michel
Trudeau's sons with Margaret Sinclair Trudeau. They were born in 1971, 1972, and 1975, respectively. The Trudeau's marriage broke down in the late 1970s, and the couple were officially divorced in 1984.

Deng Xiao Ping
Reformist leader of the People's Republic of China after Mao's death.

Ziao Zhiyang
Political leader in China.

"...Your essays, with the quotes under the titles"
Specifically, the book of essays mentioned was *Federalism and the French Canadians* (Macmillan of Canada, 1968).

Thomas Aquinas
Italian Dominican friar and priest and an influential philosopher and theologian, born in 1225.

Alexis De Tocqueville
French political philosopher and historian born in 1805.

"...The loss of your son, Michel"
The youngest son of Pierre Trudeau and his former wife, Margaret, Michel Charles Emile Trudeau, was killed in a mountain avalanche in 1998 while skiing in Kokanee Glacier Provincial Park in B.C. His body was swept into Kokanee Lake and was never recovered.

Trudeau Stories Study Guide
Stephanie Baptist

Welcome to this study guide for *Trudeau Stories* by Brooke Johnson. Whether you are studying the play in a drama class or a book club, we hope you'll find these activities enriching.

Seabreeze

1. Find a print of a photograph of yourself that is at least ten years old. Write what you recall about that moment. Who else is in the photo with you? Do you remember who took it? What is it about that image that is important for you to keep? Does having the photograph trigger memories that you might have otherwise forgotten?

Let each person share their photo and read highlights from their writing.

The Shoes

2. In this section, young Brooke Johnson asks, "why, why, *why* is he in that bag?" Brooke creates an analogy between her childhood perspective and the television news her parents were watching. She conflates Rusty the Rooster (a puppet in the CBC television program *The Friendly Giant,* who lived in a cloth bag hanging on the wall) with Pierre Laporte (the Québec Labour Minister who was kidnapped and assassinated by the FLQ (le Front de Libération du Québec) in 1970. Laporte's body was found in the trunk of a car wrapped in a sheet.

What other analogies are in this play?

Which political events do you remember from childhood? Canada's participation in the war in Afghanistan? 9/11? The fall of the Berlin Wall? Did your family discuss these events with you directly or were these topics 'not for children'? How did you sort through the confusion?

3. Have you ever met someone who is famous? When dancing with former Prime Minister Pierre Trudeau, Brooke Johnson describes him as "finely freckled", "elegant and surprisingly shy". What three traits come to mind when you describe your personal impressions of the famous person you met? Is there a difference between the persona of that famous person and how they come across in person? (Do we create the aura around someone who is famous? What is a magnetic personality?)

If you've never had a brush with celebrity, recall your first impressions of a friend. What words would you use to describe that person? How might they describe you?

Pine Avenue and **Escher's Staircase**

4. In 1985, when Pierre Trudeau met Brooke, he had left Parliament after many years, having served for over fifteen years as Prime Minister. Brooke writes, "Looking back now, I see it *was* a romance, in a *"Boy's Own"* kind of way…" *(Boy's Own* was a magazine published from the early 1800's until the mid 1900's that was intended to entertain and build character in its pre-teen, male readers.)

In characterizing our own lives, our relationships, and our identities, self-identification is more important than the labels others apply to us. What barriers exist—or what barriers do we set up for ourselves preventing us from relating to others? Do you feel that some people are of a different status than you? Why, or why not? Should status be a reason why you might not express your point of view? Does a person of so-called "higher status" have more valid ideas than you?

Try improvising a two-character scene where one character has higher status than the other. Partway through the improvisation, keep the same characters, but flip the status. How does unequal status affect the ways the characters interact?

Dark Night

5. Brooke's letter, dated "November 2nd, 1986", is full of reflections on her own life and the nature of her connection with Pierre.

"I wonder if he has ever yearned for something without knowing what it

was. I could show him the feeling: Take a sip of cognac, think of a poem. As you're thinking, swirl it in your mouth, take a tiny breath, and slowly swallow. That burning all through you—is like yearning."

Poems mentioned in *Trudeau Stories* include Brooke's "mishmash of bits of Shakespeare...and me faking him", recited in 'Tut-tut'; Yeats' "When You Are Old" and "The Second Coming", Blake's "Ah, Sunflower", Swinburne's "Chorus", and Matthew Arnold's "Dover Beach".

Read of one or all of these poems. How is yearning expressed? What word within the poem best suggests yearning? Write a "One-Minute Poem" about yearning: Set a timer for sixty seconds, and use the time to write down whatever comes to mind on the subject of yearning. Share with the group if you feel comfortable.

Tut-tut

6. The theme of friendship is explored throughout the play. In her poem, Ms. Johnson calls it a kind of "close rapport" in which we might lift "the mask we show to most." Mr. Trudeau says "my old great friends...recognize when I am 'in my shell'. In addition to "mask" and "shell", what other metaphors might we use to describe our public and private identities?

Get on your feet and see if you can find a way to physicalize the differences, if any, between your public persona and how you are when you're with a good friend, or how you are when you are alone.

Birthday Lunch

7. In 1968, at the Liberal leadership convention, Pierre Trudeau outlined his vision of Canada: "this beautiful, rich and energetic country of ours can become a model of the just society in which every citizen will enjoy his fundamental rights, in which two great linguistic communities and peoples of many cultures will live in harmony. C'est ça, le Canada."

Pierre Trudeau had a vision of one Canada, bilingual and multicultural, laid out in the Charter of Rights and Freedoms, which is the first section of the constitution, patriated in 1982 by his final government.

What's your own vision of Canada? If you were giving a toast at a Canada Day event, how would you convey your views?

Letters (1987, FTA)

8. In discussing the Free Trade Agreement, Johnson writes:

"...one possible good thing might be that we are forced to ponder what this country means to us, what we want to stand on guard for, and that we may have to fight for it. In doing so, maybe we'd collectively discover that we do have a culture—"

Brooke Johnson mentions various factors—her work in theatre as well as political negotiations—that have made her consider Canadian culture and her own Canadian identity.

Whether you are officially a citizen or not, if you consider yourself Canadian, what makes you so? Which Canadian works of art (paintings, books, movies, plays, television shows) particularly resonate with you?

Last Letter (2000)

9. In her last letter, Brooke writes:

"You are a treasure to me. We are an amalgam of people we have met along the way. And you—knowing you & having you as a friend has become a part of me. You have given me such exquisite memories and unique hope. You are a part of my imagination, a spark in my mind's eye, a spur to my confidence."

Quickly list many of the people who form the "amalgam" which is you. Read over your list and circle three names. What has each of these people given you? "Memories"? "Hope"? "Confidence"? What else?

10. In the same letter, Brooke writes Pierre:

"I kick myself for letting so much time slip by, for not maintaining contact with you, for not expressing myself, however inadequately, about the loss of your son, Michel."

In "Escher's Staircase," Pierre calls writing letters "a lost art." Since the advent of email, we write fewer letters than ever. Choose one of the three people you identified in the exercise above and use a pen and paper to write that person a letter. Express one of the following: sympathy, gratitude, regret, optimism, anxiety, or fear.

Thank you for exploring these activities as you study *Trudeau Stories*. If you have any feedback on this study guide, please contact Scirocco Drama / J. Gordon Shillingford Publishing.

Stephanie Baptist holds a Masters degree in Adult Education from the Ontario Institute for Studies in Education and a specialized B.Ed. from Queen's University called "The Artist in Community Education." She bagan her career as a theatre actor then worked with Roots of Empathy/Racines de l'empathie as a bilingual, international trainer. Stephanie, like Brooke, wants to keep talking about "wanderlust" and doing "something of consequence."

Acknowledgements

A great big thank you to David Fox for his dogged encouragement to wade through mourning by writing it down; to Julie Stewart for some key reminiscences; and to the Toronto Arts Council and Ontario Arts Council for workshop grants and the Thousand Island Playhouse for sponsoring my OAC's Theatre Creator's Reserve grant; I am grateful to Irena Malyholowka at the National Theatre School of Canada for digging through a box in the library and sending me the photograph that I'd never had.

I'd also like to acknowledge the Summerworks Theatre Festival; and Andy McKim at Theatre Passe Muraille for the 2008 remount of *Trudeau Stories,* whereupon we had the opportunity to work on the script a bit more, and for all his help in pushing it on.

I'd like to express my incalculable gratitude to Adrian Truss for coaxing and securing a first production of the play, which meant I had to actually write the script; and to my extraordinary parents, Mary and Bradley for, well, everything.